Chinua Achebe
Collected Poems

CHINUA ACHEBE was born in Nigeria in 1930. He was raised in the large village of Ogidi, one of the first centres of Anglican missionary work in eastern Nigeria, and is a graduate of University College, Ibadan.

His early career in radio ended abruptly in 1966, when he left his post as director of external broadcasting in Nigeria during the national upheaval that led to the Biafran War. He was appointed senior research fellow at the University of Nigeria, Nsukka, and began lecturing widely abroad. From 1972 to 1975, and again from 1987 to 1988, he was professor of English at the University of Massachusetts, Amherst, and also for one year at the University of Connecticut, Storrs.

Cited in the *Sunday Times* as one of the '1,000 Makers of the Twentieth Century' for defining 'a modern African literature that was truly African' and thereby making 'a major contribution to world literature', Chinua Achebe has published novels, short stories, essays, and children's books. His volume of poetry *Christmas in Biafra and Other Poems*, written during the Biafran War, was the joint winner of the first Commonwealth Poetry Prize. Of his novels, *Arrow of God* won the New Statesman–Jock Campbell Award, and *Anthills of the Savannah* was a finalist for the 1987 Booker Prize.

Chinua Achebe has received numerous honours from around the world, including the Honorary Fellowship of the American Academy of Arts and Letters and Foreign Honorary Membership of the American Academy of Arts and Sciences, as well as more than thirty honorary doctorates from universities in England, Scotland, the United States, Canada, Nigeria, and South Africa. He is also the recipient of Nigeria's highest honour for intellectual achievement, the Nigerian National Order of Merit, and of Germany's Friedenpreis des Deutschen Buchhandels for 2002.

Chinua Achebe lives with his wife in Annandale-on-Hudson, New York, where they teach at Bard College. They have four children and three grandchildren.

Also by Chinua Achebe

Anthills of the Savannah

The Sacrificial Egg and Other Stories

Things Fall Apart

No Longer at Ease

Chike and the River

A Man of the People

Arrow of God

Girls at War and Other Stories

Christmas in Biafra and Other Poems

Beware Soul Brother

Morning Yet on Creation Day

The Trouble with Nigeria

The Flute

The Drum

Hopes and Impediments

How the Leopard Got His Claws (with John Iroaganachi)

Winds of Change: Modern Short Stories
from Black Africa (with others)

African Short Stories (editor, with C. L. Innes)

Another Africa (with Robert Lyons)

Home and Exile

Collected Poems

Chinua Achebe

CARCANET

Acknowledgements

The poem 'Mango Seedling' was first published in *The New York Review of Books* in 1968 and was dedicated to the memory of the poet Christopher Okigbo. 'Those Gods Are Children' first appeared in somewhat different form in *The Conch*, 'Love Song (for Anna)' in *Zuka*, 'Their Idiot Song' in *Transition*, 'Knowing Robs Us' and 'The Nigerian Census' in *Callaloo*, and 'Flying', 'Agostinho Neto' and 'The Pine Tree in Spring' in . A good number of the others have appeared in *Okike: An African Journal of New Writing* and in *Christmas in Biafra and Other Poems*.

First published in Great Britain in 2005 by
Carcanet Press Limited
Alliance House
Cross Street
Manchester M2 7AQ

First published in the United States by Anchor Books,
a division of Random House, Inc., New York

A CIP catalogue record for this book is available from the British Library
ISBN 1 85754 843 4

The publisher acknowledges financial assistance from Arts Council England

Printed and bound in England by SRP Ltd, Exeter

To the Memory of My Mother

Contents

CONTENTS

In Lieu of a Preface: A Parable

The Author had begun to worry about his own conduct. Perhaps he had not been fair to his poems. Yes, the same poetry that had surged from the depths to bring pain-soaked solace in the breach and darkness of civil war. Now he had stepped out alone into the light.

Everyone knows, of course, that an author cannot possibly bring things to such a pass unaided. He had plenty of help from his then Publisher, who filled the role of primary culprit, leaving the Author with the guilt only of acquiescence and quietude. For, in truth, the Author had raised the matter of his poems now and again with the Publisher, aloof in his towers and battlements in distant London, unready for strange images and cadences; and his reply had always been a telegraphic non sequitur: We do very well with your novels, you know.

In time the poems, like all children reared in hardship, grew tougher and wiser than their peers. They figured out that as offspring of a heedless parent they were fated to find their own way in the world. Their unguided wandering before long brought them face-to-face with a magician, Negative Capability, *the holy man of the forest, shaggy-haired powered for eternal replenishment*, alias Man Pass Man; and he blessed their struggle.

They went out early one morning in search of validation and returned at nightfall singing and dancing and bearing aloft the trophy of Commonwealth Poetry. A few ripples, but no waves. They contrived something breathtakingly audacious: they got Her Britannic Majesty to invoke six of their lines to end a royal admonition to her Commonwealth in crisis. *Remember also your children for they in their time . . .*

More ripples, but hardly any waves. If the Publisher heard any of it he kept the news to himself, and kept also his blurb on the book of poems in which he absentmindedly praised the novels.

What happened next is not very clear, though there is no lack of speculation. The one certain fact, however, is that the poems went silent. Did they go underground, as one rather romantic commentator would have it, to cultivate a secret guild of readers? Nobody can really say. The Author does recall, however, that at about this time he had begun to observe increasing numbers of intense-looking men and women in his audiences who would go up to the dais at the end of a reading and ask—or even demand—to know where to find the book he read from.

An American photographer with a fine portfolio of African material came on the scene at this time with a request to the Author for collaboration. So impressed was the Author by the photographs that he readily agreed to contribute to a catalog of their exhibition, and became joint author of a magnificent coffee-table book with the beguiling title of *Another Africa*. In his enthusiasm he found himself traveling across the United States to Seattle and Portland, Oregon, to read and speak at the exhibition.

And then things took a sudden, unexpected turn. The Author received an urgent call from a lady who identified herself as Curator of *Another Africa* exhibition, now showing in a major museum in the Midwest, in a city that had better remain nameless. She wanted to know from the Author how she might get hold of his book of poems in a hurry.

- Why in a hurry?
- Because visitors to the exhibition are taking away
  your poems from the catalog.
- Taking away my poems, how?
- Ripping them out. And carrying them away.
- My gentle readers? Oh, dear!
- What's that?
- Never mind.

The Author has at last found a new Publisher who, unaware of these events, has set about publishing his collected poems. The Author, suitably chastened, is dreaming of a new day when peace will return to the affair of books, to wit: writing, publishing, and reading.

Prologue

Prologue

1966

absentminded
our thoughtless days
sat at dire controls
and played indolently

slowly downward in remote
subterranean shaft
a diamond-tipped
drill point crept closer
to residual chaos to
rare artesian hatred
that once squirted warm
blood in God's face
confirming His first
disappointment in Eden

Nsukka, November 19, 1971

CHINUA ACHEBE

Benin Road

Speed is violence
Power is violence
Weight violence

The butterfly seeks safety in lightness
In weightless, undulating flight

But at a crossroads where mottled light
From old trees falls on a brash new highway
Our separate errands collide

I come power-packed for two
And the gentle butterfly offers
Itself in bright yellow sacrifice
Upon my hard silicon shield.

Mango Seedling

Through glass windowpane
Up a modern office block
I saw, two floors below, on wide-jutting
concrete canopy a mango seedling newly sprouted
Purple, two-leafed, standing on its burst
Black yolk. It waved brightly to sun and wind
Between rains—daily regaling itself
On seed yams, prodigally.
For how long?
How long the happy waving
From precipice of rainswept sarcophagus?
How long the feast on remnant flour
At pot bottom?
      Perhaps like the widow
Of infinite faith it stood in wait
For the holy man of the forest, shaggy-haired
Powered for eternal replenishment.
Or else it hoped for Old Tortoise's miraculous feast
On one ever recurring dot of cocoyam
Set in a large bowl of green vegetables—
This day beyond fable, beyond faith?
      Then I saw it
Poised in courageous impartiality
Between the primordial quarrel of Earth

And Sky striving bravely to sink roots
Into objectivity, midair in stone.

I thought the rain, prime mover
To this enterprise, someday would rise in power
And deliver its ward in delirious waterfall
Toward earth below. But every rainy day
Little playful floods assembled on the slab,
Danced, parted round its feet,
United again, and passed.
It went from purple to sickly green
Before it died.
        Today I see it still—
Dry, wire-thin in sun and dust of the dry months—
Headstone on tiny debris of passionate courage.

Aba, 1968

Pine Tree in Spring

(for Leon Damas)

Pine tree
flag bearer
of green memory
across the breach of a desolate hour

Loyal tree
that stood guard
alone in austere emeraldry
over Nature's recumbent standard

Pine tree
lost now in the shade
of traitors decked out flamboyantly
marching back unabashed to the colors they betrayed

Fine tree
erect and trustworthy
what school can teach me
your silent, stubborn fidelity?

The Explorer

Like a dawn unheralded at midnight
it opened abruptly before me—a rough
circular clearing, high cliffs of deep
forest guarding it in amber-tinted spell

A long journey's end it was though how
long and from where seemed unclear,
unimportant; one fact alone mattered
now—that body so well preserved
which on seeing I knew had brought me there

The circumstance of death
was vague but a floating hint
pointed to a disaster in the air
elusively

But where, if so, the litter
of violent wreckage? That rough-edged
gypsum trough bearing it like a dead
chrysalis reposing till now in full
encapsulation was broken by a cool
hand for this lying in state. All else
was in order except the leg missing
neatly at knee joint

even the white schoolboy dress
immaculate in the thin yellow
light; the face in particular
was perfect having caught nor fear
nor agony at the fatal moment.

Clear-sighted with a clarity
rarely encountered in dreams
my Explorer-Self stood a little
distant but somewhat fulfilled; behind
him a long misty quest: unanswered
questions put to sleep needing
no longer to be raised. Enough
in that trapped silence of a freak
dawn to come face-to-face suddenly
with a body I didn't even know
I lost.

Agostinho Neto

Neto, were you no more
Than the middle one favored by fortune
In children's riddle; Kwame
Striding ahead to accost
Demons; behind you a laggard third
As yet unnamed, of twisted fingers?

No! Your secure strides
Were hard earned. Your feet
Learned their fierce balance
In violent slopes of humiliation;
Your delicate hands, patiently
Groomed for finest incisions,
Were commandeered brusquely to kill,
Your melodious voice to battle cry.

Perhaps your family and friends
Knew a merry flash cracking the gloom
We see in pictures but I prefer
And will keep the darker legend.
For I have seen how
Half a millennium of alien rape
And murder can stamp a smile
On the vacant face of the fool,

The sinister grin of Africa's idiot-kings
Who oversee in obscene palaces of gold
The butchery of their own people.

Neto, I sing your passing, I,
Timid requisitioner of your vast
Armory's most congenial supply.
What shall I sing? A dirge answering
The gloom? No, I will sing tearful songs
Of joy; I will celebrate
The Man who rode a trinity
Of awesome fates to the cause
Of our trampled race!
Thou Healer, Soldier, and Poet!

Poems About War

The First Shot

That lone rifle-shot anonymous
in the dark striding chest-high
through a nervous suburb at the break
of our season of thunders will yet
steep its flight and lodge
more firmly than the greater noises
ahead in the forehead of memory.

CHINUA ACHEBE

A Mother in a Refugee Camp

No Madonna and Child could touch
Her tenderness for a son
She soon would have to forget. . . .
The air was heavy with odors of diarrhea,
Of unwashed children with washed-out ribs
And dried-up bottoms waddling in labored steps
Behind blown-empty bellies. Other mothers there
Had long ceased to care, but not this one:
She held a ghost-smile between her teeth,
And in her eyes the memory
Of a mother's pride. . . . She had bathed him
And rubbed him down with bare palms.
She took from their bundle of possessions
A broken comb and combed
The rust-colored hair left on his skull
And then—humming in her eyes—began carefully to part it.
In their former life this was perhaps
A little daily act of no consequence
Before his breakfast and school; now she did it
Like putting flowers on a tiny grave.

Christmas in Biafra (1969)

This sunken-eyed moment wobbling
down the rocky steepness on broken
bones slowly fearfully to hideous
concourse of gathering sorrows in the valley
will yet become in another year a lost
Christmas irretrievable in the heights
its exploding inferno transmuted
by cosmic distances to the peacefulness
of a cool twinkling star. . . . To death-cells
of that moment came faraway sounds of other
men's carols floating on crackling waves
mocking us. With regret? Hope? Longing? None of
these, strangely, not even despair rather
distilling pure transcendental hate . . .

Beyond the hospital gate
the good nuns had set up a manger
of palms to house a fine plastercast
scene at Bethlehem. The Holy
Family was central, serene, the Child
Jesus plump wise-looking and rose-cheeked; one
of the magi in keeping with legend
a black Othello in sumptuous robes. Other
figures of men and angels stood

at well-appointed distances from
the heart of the divine miracle
and the usual cattle gazed on
in holy wonder. . . .

Poorer than the poor worshippers
before her who had paid their homage
with pitiful offering of new aluminum
coins that few traders would take and
a frayed five-shilling note she only
crossed herself and prayed open-eyed. Her
infant son flat like a dead lizard
on her shoulder his arms and legs
cauterized by famine was a miracle
of its kind. Large sunken eyes
stricken past boredom to a flat
unrecognizing glueyness moped faraway
motionless across her shoulder. . . .

Now her adoration over
she turned him around and pointed
at those pretty figures of God
and angels and men and beasts—
a spectacle to stir the heart
of a child. But all he vouchsafed
was one slow deadpan look of total
unrecognition and he began again
to swivel his enormous head away
to mope as before at his empty distance. . . .
She shrugged her shoulders, crossed
herself again, and took him away.

Air Raid

It comes so quickly
the bird of death
from evil forests of Soviet technology

A man crossing the road
to greet a friend
is much too slow.
His friend cut in halves
has other worries now
than a friendly handshake
at noon.

Biafra, 1969

First time Biafra
Was here, we're told, it was a fine
Figure massively hewn in hardwood.

Voracious white ants
Set upon it and ate
Through its huge emplaced feet
To the great heart abandoning
A furrowed, emptied scarecrow.

And sun-stricken waves came and beat crazily
About its feet eaten hollow
Till crashing facedown in a million fragments
It was floated gleefully away
To cold shores—cartographers alone
Marking the coastline
Of that forgotten massive stance.

In our time it came again
In pain and acrid smell
Of powder. And furious wreckers
Emboldened by half a millennium
Of conquest, battening
On new oil dividends, are now

At its black throat squeezing
Blood and lymph down to
Its hands and feet
Bloated by quashiokor.

Must Africa have
To come a third time?

An "If" of History

Just think, had Hitler won
his war the mess our history
books would be today. The Americans
flushed by verdict of victory
hanged a Japanese commander for
war crimes. A generation later
an itching finger pokes their ribs:
> We've got to hang
> our Westmoreland
> for bloodier crimes
> in Viet Nam!
But everyone by now must
know that hanging takes much more
than a victim no matter his
load of manifest guilt. For even
in lynching a judge of sorts is needed—
a winner. Just think if Hitler
had gambled and won what chaos
the world would have known. His
implacable foe across the Channel
would surely have died for
war crimes. And as for H. Truman,
the Hiroshima villain, well!
Had Hitler won his war

de Gaulle would have needed no
further trial for was he not
condemned already by Paris
to die for his treason
to France? . . . Had Hitler won,
Vidkun Quisling would have kept
his job as Prime Minister
of Norway, simply by
Hitler winning.

CHINUA ACHEBE

Remembrance Day

Your proclaimed mourning
your flag at half-mast your
solemn face your smart backward
step and salute at the flowered
foot of empty graves your
glorious words—none, nothing
will their spirit appease. Had they
the choice they would gladly
have worn for you the same
stricken face gladly flown
your droopéd flag spoken
your tremulous eulogy—and
been alive. . . . Admittedly you
suffered too. You lived wretchedly
on all manner of gross fare;
you were tethered to the nervous
precipice day and night; your
groomed hair lost gloss, your
smooth body roundedness. Truly
you suffered much. But now
you have the choice of a dozen
ways to rehabilitate yourself.
Pick any one of them and soon
you will forget the fear

and hardship, the peril
on the edge of the chasm. . . . The
shops stock again a variety
of hair dyes, the lace and
the gold are coming back; so
you will regain lost mirth
and girth and forget. But when,
how soon, will they their death? Long,
long after you forget they turned
newcomers again before the hazards
and rigors of reincarnation, rude
clods once more who once had borne
the finest scarifications of the potter's
delicate hand now squashed back
into primeval mud, they will
remember. Therefore fear them! Fear
their malice your fallen kindred
wronged in death. Fear their blood feud;
tremble for the day of their
visit! Flee! Flee! Flee your
guilt palaces and cities! Flee
lest they come to ransack
your place and find you still
at home at the crossroad hour. Pray
that they return empty-handed
that day to nurse their red-hot
hatred for another long year. . . .
Your glorious words are not
for them nor your proliferation
in a dozen cities of the bronze
heroes of Idumota. . . . Flee! Seek
asylum in distant places till

a new generation of heroes rise
in phalanges behind their purified
child-priest to inaugurate
a season of atonement and rescue
from fingers calloused by heavy deeds
the tender rites of reconciliation

A Wake for Okigbo

For whom are we searching?
For whom are we searching?
For Okigbo we are searching!

                Nzomalizo!

Has he gone for firewood, let him return.
Has he gone to fetch water, let him return.
Has he gone to the marketplace, let him return.
For Okigbo we are searching.

                Nzomalizo!

For whom are we searching?
For whom are we searching?
For Okigbo we are searching!

                Nzomalizo!

Has he gone for firewood, may Ugboko not take him.
Has he gone to the stream, may Iyi not swallow him!
Has he gone to the market, then keep from him you
    Tumult of the marketplace!
Has he gone to battle,
    please Ogbonuke step aside for him!
For Okigbo we are searching!

                Nzomalizo!

They bring home a dance, who is to dance it for us?
They bring home a war, who will fight it for us?
The one we call repeatedly,
 there's something he alone can do
It is Okigbo we are calling!
       Nzomalizo!

Witness the dance, how it arrives
The war, how it has broken out
But the caller of the dance is nowhere to be found
The brave one in battle is nowhere in sight!
Do you not see now that whom we call again
And again, there is something he alone can do?
It is Okigbo we are calling!
       Nzomalizo!

The dance ends abruptly
The spirit dancers fold their dance and depart in midday
Rain soaks the stalwart, soaks the two-sided drum!
The flute is broken that elevates the spirit
The music pot shattered that accompanies the leg in
 its measure
Brave one of my blood!
Brave one of Igbo land!
Brave one in the middle of so much blood!
Owner of riches in the dwelling place of spirit
Okigbo is the one I am calling!
       Nzomalizo!

In memory of the poet Christopher Okigbo (1932–1967)
Translated from the Igbo by Ifeanyi Menkiti

After a War

After a war life catches
desperately at passing
hints of normalcy like
vines entwining a hollow
twig; its famished roots
close on rubble and every
piece of broken glass.

Irritations we used
to curse return to joyous
tables like prodigals home
from the city. . . . The meter man
serving my maiden bill brought
a friendly face to my circle
of sullen strangers and me
smiling gratefully
to the door.

After a war
we clutch at watery
scum pulsating on listless
eddies of our spent
deluge. . . . Convalescent
dancers rising too soon

to rejoin their circle dance
our powerless feet intent
as before but no longer
adept contrive only
half-remembered
eccentric steps.

After years
of pressing death
and dizzy last-hour reprieves
we're glad to dump our fears
and our perilous gains together
in one shallow grave and flee
the same rueful way we came
straight home to haunted revelry.

Christmas 1971

Poems Not About War

Love Song (for Anna)

Bear with me my love
in the hour of my silence;
the air is crisscrossed
by loud omens and songbirds
fearing reprisals of middle day
have hidden away their notes
wrapped up in leaves
of cocoyam. . . . What song shall I
sing to you my love when
a choir of squatting toads
turns the stomach of day with
goitrous adoration of an infested
swamp and purple-headed
vultures at home stand
sentry on the rooftop?

I will sing only in waiting
silence your power to bear
my dream for me in your quiet
eyes and wrap the dust of our blistered
feet in golden anklets ready
for the return someday of our
banished dance.

Love Cycle

At dawn slowly
the Sun withdraws his
long misty arms of
embrace. Happy lovers
whose exertions leave
no aftertaste nor slush
of love's combustion; Earth
perfumed in dewdrop
fragrance wakes
to whispers of
soft-eyed light. . . .
    Later he
will wear out his temper
plowing the vast acres
of heaven and take it
out on her in burning
darts of anger. Long
accustomed to such caprice
she waits patiently
for evening when thoughts
of another night will
restore his mellowness
and her power
over him.

Question

Angled sunbeam lowered
like Jacob's ladder through
sky's peephole pierced in the roof
to my silent floor and bared feet.
Are these your creatures
these crowding specks
stomping your lighted corridor
to a remote sun, like doped
acrobatic angels gyrating
at needlepoint to divert a high
unamused god? Or am I
sole stranger in a twilight room
I called my own overrun
and possessed long ago by myriads more
as yet invisible in all
this surrounding penumbra?

Answer

I broke at last
the terror-fringed fascination
that bound my ancient gaze
to those crowding faces
of plunder and seized my
remnant life in a miracle
of decision between white-
collar hands and shook it
like a cheap watch in
my ear and threw it down
beside me on the earth floor
and rose to my feet. I
made of their shoulders
and heads bobbing up and down
a new ladder and leaned
it on their sweating flanks
and ascended till midair
my hands so new to harshness
could grapple the roughness of a prickly
day and quench the source
that fed turbulence to their
feet. I made a dramatic
descent that day landing
backways into crouching shadows

into potsherds of broken trance. I
flung open long-disused windows
and doors and saw my hut
new-swept by rainbow brooms
of sunlight become my home again
on whose trysting floor waited
my proud vibrant life.

CHINUA ACHEBE

Beware, Soul Brother

We are the men of soul
men of song we measure out
our joys and agonies
too, our long, long passion week
in paces of the dance. We have
come to know from surfeit of suffering
that even the Cross need not be
a dead end nor total loss
if we should go to it striding
the dirge of the soulful *abia* drums. . . .
        But beware soul brother
of the lures of ascension day
the day of soporific levitation
on high winds of skysong; beware
for others there will be that day
lying in wait leaden-footed, tone-deaf
passionate only for the deep entrails
of our soil; beware of the day
we head truly skyward leaving
that spoil to the long ravenous tooth
and talon of their hunger.
Our ancestors, soul brother, were wiser
than is often made out. Remember
they gave Ala, great goddess

38

of their earth, sovereignty too over
their arts for they understood
so well those hardheaded
men of departed dance where a man's
foot must return whatever beauties
it may weave in air, where
it must return for safety
and renewal of strength. Take care
then, mother's son, lest you become
a dancer disinherited in mid-dance
hanging a lame foot in air like the hen
in a strange unfamiliar compound. Pray
protect this patrimony to which
you must return when the song
is finished and the dancers disperse;
remember also your children
for they in their time will want
a place for their feet when
they come of age and the dance
of the future is born
for them.

CHINUA ACHEBE

NON-commitment

Hurrah! to them who do nothing
see nothing feel nothing whose
hearts are fitted with prudence
like a diaphragm across
womb's beckoning doorway to bar
the scandal of seminal rage. I'm
told the owl too wears wisdom
in a ring of defense round
each vulnerable eye securing it fast
against the darts of sight. Long ago
in the Middle East Pontius Pilate
openly washed involvement off his
white hands and became famous. (Of all
the Roman officials before him and after
who else is talked about
every Sunday in the Apostles' Creed?) And
talking of apostles that other fellow
Judas wasn't such a fool
either; though much maligned by
succeeding generations the fact remains
he alone in that motley crowd
had sense enough to tell a doomed
movement when he saw one
and get out quick, a nice little

40

packet bulging his coat pocket
into the bargain—sensible fellow.

September 1970

Generation Gap

A son's arrival
is the crescent moon
too new too soon to lodge
the man's returning. His
feast of reincarnation
must await the moon's
ripening at the naming
ceremony of his
grandson.

Misunderstanding

My old man had a little saying
he loved and as he neared
his end was prone to relish
more and more. Wherever Something
stands, he'd say, there also Something
Else will stand. Heedless at first
I waved it aside as mere
elderly prattle that youth have to bear
till sharply one day it hit home to me
that never before, not even
once, did I hear mother speak
again in their little disputes once
he'd said it. From then began
my long unrest: what was this
Thing so unanswerable and why
was it dogged by that
relentless Other? My mother
proved no help at all nor did
my father whose sole reply
was just a solemn smile. . . . Quietly
later of its own will it showed
its face, so slowly, to me though
not before they'd long been dead—my
little old man and my mother

also—and showed me too how
utterly vain my private quest
had been. Flushed by success
I spoke one day in a trifling
row: you see, my darling (to
my wife) where Something
stands—no matter what—there
Something Else will take its
stand. I knew, she said; she
pouted her lips like a gun
in my face. She knew, she said,
she'd known all along of that
other woman I was keeping in town.
And I fear, my friends,
I am yet to hear
the last of it.

Knowing Robs Us

Knowing robs us of wonder.
Had it not ripped apart
the fearful robes of primordial Night
to steal the design that crafted horns
on doghead and sowed insurrection
overnight in the homely beak
of a hen; had reason not given us
assurance that day will daily break
and the sun's array return to disarm
night's fantastic figurations—
each daybreak
would be garlanded at the city gate
and escorted with royal drums
to a stupendous festival
of an amazed world.

One day
after the passage of a dark April storm
ecstatic birds followed its furrows
sowing songs of daybreak though the time
was now past noon, their sparkling
notes sprouting green incantations
everywhere to free the world
from harmattan death.

But for me
the celebration is make-believe;
the clamorous change of season
will darken the hills of Nsukka
for an hour or two when it comes;
no hurricane will hit my sky—
and no song of deliverance.

Bull and Egret

At seventy miles an hour
one morning down the seesaw
road to Nsukka I came
upon a mighty bull
in form and carriage
so unlike Fulani cattle—
gaunt, high-horned, triangular
faced—that come in herded
multitudes from dusty savannas
to the north. . . . Heavy
was he, solitary dark
and taciturn, one of a tribe
they say fate has chosen
for slow extinction. At his heels
paced his egret, intent
praise-singer, pure white
all neck, walking high
stilts and yet no higher
than his master's leg joint. . . .
Odd covetousness indeed would
leave its boundless green estates
for a spell of petty trespassing
on perilous asphalt laid for me. . . . My
frantic blast of iron voice

shattered their stately march, then
recoiled brutally to my heart
as he gathered in hasty panic
the heaviness of his hind-
quarters, so ungainly in his
hurry, and flung it desperate
beyond my monstrous
reach. I should have felt unworthy then
playing such pranks on the noble
elder and watching his hallowed
waist cloth came undone had not
his singer fared so well. . . . Two
quick hops, a flap of
wings and he was
safe posture intact on
brown laterite. . . . I could not
bear him playing so
faithfully my faithless agility-man, my
scrambler to safety, throat dilated
still by remnant praises
of his excellency high-headed
in delusion marching now alone
into death's ambush. . . . We were
spared, the bull and I, in our separate follies. . . .
His routed sunrise procession
no doubt would reform beyond the clamor
of my passage and sprightly
egret take up again
his broken adulation
of the bull, his everlasting
prince, his giver-in-abundance
of heavenly cattle ticks.

Lazarus

We know the breathtaking
joy of his sisters when the word
spread: He is risen! But a
man who has lived a full life
will have others to
reckon with beside his
sisters. Certainly that keen-eyed
assistant who has moved up
to his table at the office, for
him resurrection is an awful
embarrassment. . . . The luckless
people of Ogbaku knew its
terrors that day the twin-headed
evil strode their highway. It
could not have been easy
picking up again the blood-spattered
clubs they had cast away; or to
turn from the battered body
of the barrister lying beside his
battered limousine to finish off
their own man, stirring now suddenly
in wide-eyed resurrection. . . . How well
they understood, those grim-faced
villagers wielding their crimson

weapons once more, how well
they understood that at the hour
of his rising their kinsman
avenged in murder would turn
away from them in obedience
to other fraternities, would turn indeed
their own accuser and in one
breath obliterate their plea
and justification! So they killed
him a second time that day on the
threshold of a promising resurrection.

Vultures

In the grayness
and drizzle of one despondent
dawn unstirred by harbingers
of sunbreak a vulture
perching high on broken
bone of a dead tree
nestled close to his
mate his smooth
bashed-in head, a pebble
on a stem rooted in
a dump of gross
feathers, inclined affectionately
to hers. Yesterday they picked
the eyes of a swollen
corpse in a waterlogged
trench and ate the
things in its bowel. Full
gorged they chose their roost
keeping the hollowed remnant
in easy range of cold
telescopic eyes. . . .
        Strange
indeed how love in other
ways so particular

will pick a corner
in that charnel house
tidy it and coil up there, perhaps
even fall asleep—her face
turned to the wall!
. . . Thus the Commandant at Belsen
Camp going home for
the day with fumes of
human roast clinging
rebelliously to his hairy
nostrils will stop
at the wayside sweetshop
and pick up a chocolate
for his tender offspring
waiting at home for Daddy's
return. . . .
     Praise bounteous
providence if you will
that grants even an ogre
its glowworm
tenderness encapsulated
in icy caverns of a cruel
heart or else despair
for in the very germ
of that kindred love is
lodged the perpetuity
of evil.

Public Execution in Pictures

The caption did not overlook
the smart attire of the squad. Certainly
there was impressive swagger in that
ready, high-elbowed stance; belted
and sashed in threaded dragon teeth
they waited in self-imposed restraint—
fine ornament on power unassailable—
for their cue

        at the crucial time
this pretty close-up lady in fine lace
proved unequal to it, her first no doubt,
and quickly turned away. But not
this other—her face, rigid
in pain, firmly held between her palms;
though not perfect yet, it seems
clear she has put the worst
behind her today

        in my home
far from the crowded live-show
on the hot, bleached sands of Victoria
Beach my little kids will crowd
round our Sunday paper and debate

hotly why the heads of dead
robbers always slump forward
or sideways.

Gods, Men, and Others

Penalty of Godhead

The old man's bed
of straw caught a flame blown
from overnight logs by harmattan's
incendiary breath. Defying his age and
sickness he rose and steered himself
smoke-blind to safety.

A nimble rat appeared at the
door of his hole looked quickly to left and
right and scurried across the floor
to nearby farmlands.

Even roaches that grim
tenantry that nothing discourages
fled their crevices that day on wings they
only use in deadly haste.

Household gods alone
frozen in ritual black with blood
of endless tribute festooned in feathers
perished in the blazing pyre
of that hut.

Those Gods Are Children
(for Gabriel Okara)

No man who loves himself
will dare to drink
before his fathers' presences enshrined
by the threshold have drunk
their fill. A fool alone will
contest the precedence of ancestors
and gods; the wise wisely
sing them grandiloquent lullabies
knowing they are children
those omnipotent deities.
Take that avid-eyed old man
full horn in veined hand
unsteadied by age who calls
forward his fathers tilting the horn
with amazing skill for a hand
so tremulous till grudging trickles
break through white froth
at the brim and course down
the curved side to fine point
of sacrifice ant-hole-size in earth:
> *come together all-powerful spirits*
> *and drink; no need to scramble*
> *there's enough for all!*
Or when the offering of yams

is due who sends the lively
errand son to scour the barn
and bring a sacrifice fit
for the mighty dead! Naive
eager to excel the child
returns in sweat lumbering
the heavy pride of his father's harvest:
> *ignorant child, all ears and no eyes!*
> *is that the biggest in my barn?*
> *I said the biggest!*
Only then does the nimble child
perceive a surreptitious fist quickly shown
and withdrawn again—and break through
wisdom's lashing cordon to welcoming smiles
of initiation. He makes the journey
of the neophyte to bring home a ritual
offering as big as an egg.

II

Long ago a man of fury drawn
by doom's insistent call slew
his brother. The land and every deity
screamed revenge: a head for a head
and raised their spear
to smite the town should it
withhold the due. The man
was ready. The elders' council
looked at him and turned
from him to all the orphans doubly
doomed and shook their heads:

> the gods are right and just! This man
> shall hang but first may he
> retrieve the sagging house
> of his fathers

and the fine points
of the gods' spears
returned to earth

and he lived for years that man
of death he raised his orphans

60

he worked his homestead and his farmlands
till evening came and laid him low
with cruel foraging fever. Patient
elders peering through the hut's dim
light darkened more by smoke
of smoldering fire under his bed
steady-eyed at a guilt they had stalked
across scrublands and seven rivers, a long-prepared
hangman's loop in their hand
quickly circled his neck
as he died

and the gods
and ancestors
were satisfied.

III

They are strong and to be feared
they make the mighty crash
in ruin like *iroko*'s fall
at height of noon scattering
nests and frantic birdsong
in damped silence of deep
undergrowth. Yet they are fooled
as easily as children those deities
their simple omnipotence
drowsed by praise.

Lament of the Sacred Python

I was there when lizards
were ones and twos, child
Of ancient river god Idemili. Painful
Teardrops of Sky's first weeping
Drew my spots. Sky-born
I walked the earth with royal gait
And crowds of human mourners
Filing down funereal paths
Across lengthening shadows
Of the dead acknowledged my face
In broken dirges of fear.

But of late
A wandering god pursued,
It seems, by hideous things
He did at home has come to us
And pitched his tent here
Beneath the people's holy tree
And hoisted from its pinnacle
A charlatan bell that calls
Unknown monotones of revolts,
Scandals, and false immunities.
And I that none before could meet except
In fear though I brought no terrors

From creation's day of gifts I must now
Turn on my track
In dishonorable flight
Where children stop their play
To shriek in my ringing ears:
        Look out, python! Look out, python!
        Christians relish python flesh!

And mighty god Idemili
That once upheld from earth foundations
Cloud banks of sky's endless waters
Is betrayed in his shrine by empty men
Suborned with the stranger's tawdry gifts
And taken trussed up to the altar-shrine turned
Slaughterhouse for the gory advent
Feast of an errant cannibal god
Tooth-filed to eat his fellows.

And the sky recedes in
Disgust; the orphan snake
Abandoned weeps in the shadows.

Their Idiot Song

These fellows, the old pagan
said, surely are out of their mind—
that old proudly impervious
derelict skirted long ago by floodwaters
of salvation: Behold the great
and gory handiwork of Death displayed
for all on dazzling sheets this
hour of day its twin nostrils
plugged firmly with stoppers of wool
and they ask of him: Where
is thy sting?
    Sing on, good fellows, sing
on! Someday when it is you
he decks out on his great
iron bed with cotton wool
for your breath, his massing odors
mocking your pitiful makeshift defenses
of face powder and township ladies' lascivious
scent, these others roaming
yet his roomy chicken coop will
be singing and asking still
but YOU by then
no longer will be
in doubt!

The Nigerian Census

I will not mourn with you
your lost populations, the silent columns
of your fief erased
from the king's book of numbers

For in your house of stone
by the great road
you listened once to refugee voices
at dawn telling of massacres and plagues
in their land across seven rivers

Like a hornbill in flight
you tucked in your slippered feet
from the threshold
out of their beseeching gaze

But pestilence farther
than faraway tales of dawn
had bought a seat in Ogun's reckless
chariot and knocks by nightfall
on your iron gate.

Take heart oh chief; decimation
by miscount, however grievous,

is a happy retreat from bolder
uses of the past. Take heart,
for these scribal flourishes
behind smudged entries, these
trophied returns of clerical headhunters
can never match the quiet flow
of red blood.

But if my grudging comfort fail,
then take this long and even view to A.D. 2010
when the word is due to go out again
and—depending on which Caesar
orders the count—new conurbations
may sprout in today's wastelands,
and thriving cities dissolve
in sudden mirages

and the ready-reckoners at court
will calculate their gain
and our loss, and make us
any-number-of-million-they-like strong!

Flying

(for Niyi Osundare)

Something in altitude kindles power-thirst
Mere horse-height suffices the emir
Bestowing from rich folds of prodigious turban
Upon crawling peasants in the dust
Rare imperceptible nods enwrapped
In princely boredom.

I too have known
A parching of that primordial palate,
A quickening to manifest life
Of a long recessive appetite.
Though strapped and manacled
That day I commanded from the pinnacle
Of a three-tiered world a bridge befitting
The proud deranged deity I had become.
A magic rug of rushing clouds
Billowed and rubbed its white softness
Like practiced houri fingers on my sole
And through filters of its gauzy fabric
Revealed wonders of a metropolis
Magic-struck to fairyland proportions.
By different adjustments of vision
I caused the clouds to float
Over a stilled landscape, over towers

And masts and smoke-plumed chimneys;
Or turned the very earth, unleashed
From itself, a roaming fugitive
Beneath a constant sky. Then came
A sudden brightness over the world,
A rare winter's smile it was, and printed
On my cloud carpet a black cross
Set in an orb of rainbows. To which
Splendid nativity came—who else would come
But gray unsporting Reason, faithless
Pedant offering a bald refractory annunciation?
But oh what beauty! What speed!
A chariot of night in panic flight
From Our Royal Proclamation of the rites
Of day! And riding out Our procession
Of fantasy We slaked an ancient
Vestigial greed shriveled by ages of dormancy
Till the eyes exhausted by glorious pageantries
Returned to rest on that puny
Legend of the life jacket stowed away
Of all places under my seat.

Now I think I know why gods
Are so partial to heights—to mountain
Tops and spires, to proud *iroko* trees
And thorn-guarded holy bombax,
Why petty household divinities
Will sooner perch on a rude board
Strung precariously from brittle rafters
Of a thatched roof than sit squarely
On safe earth.

Epilogue

He Loves Me; He Loves Me Not

"Harold Wilson he loves
me he gave me
a gun in my time
of need to shoot
my rebellious brother. Edward
Heath he loves
me not he's promised a gun
to his sharpshooting
brother viewing me
crazily through ramparts
of white Pretoria. . . . It
would be awful
if he got me." It was
awful and he got
him. They headlined it
on the BBC spreading
indignation through the
world, later that day
in emergency meeting his
good friend Wilson and Heath
his enemy crossed swords
over him at West-
minster and sent post-
haste Sir Alec to Africa
for the funeral.

CHINUA ACHEBE

Dereliction

I quit the carved stool
in my father's hut to the swelling
chant of saber-tooth termites
raising in the pith of its wood
a white-bellied stalagmite

Where does a runner go
whose oily grip drops
the baton handed by the faithful one
in a hard, merciless race? Or
the priestly elder who barters
for the curio collector's head
of tobacco the holy staff
of his people?

Let them try the land
where the sea retreats
Let them try the land
where the sea retreats

We Laughed at Him

We laughed at him our
hungry-eyed fool-man with itching
fingers who would see farther
than all. We called him
visionary missionary revolutionary
and, you know, all the other
naries that plague the peace, but
nothing would deter him.

With his own nails he cut
his eyes, scraped the crust
over them peeled off his priceless
patina of rest and the dormant
fury of his dammed pond
broke into a cataract
of blood tumbling down
his face and chest. . . . We
laughed at his screams the fool-man
who would see what eyes
are forbidden, the hungry-eyed
man, the look-look man, the
itching man bent to drag
into daylight fearful signs
hidden away for our safety
at the creation of the world.

He was always against
blindness, you know, our quiet
sober blindness, our lazy—he called
it—blindness. And for
his pains? A turbulent, torrential
cascading blindness behind
a Congo river of blood. He sat
backstage then behind his flaming red
curtain and groaned in
the pain his fingers unlocked, in the
rainstorm of blows loosed on his head
by the wild avenging demons he
drummed free from the silence of their
drum-house, his prize for big-eyed greed.
We sought by laughter to drown
his anguish until one day
at height of noon his screams
turned suddenly to hymns
of ecstasy. We knew then his pain
had risen to the brain
and we took pity on him
the poor fool-man as he held
converse with himself. *My Lord,*
we heard him say to the curtain
of his blood *I come to touch
the hem of your crimson robe.*
He went stark mad thereafter
raving about new sights he
claimed to see, poor fellow; sights
you and I know are as impossible for this world
to show as for a hen to urinate—if one
may borrow one of his many crazy vulgarisms—

he raved about trees topped with
green and birds flying—yes actually
flying through the air—about
the Sun and the Moon and stars
and about lizards crawling on all
fours. . . . But nobody worries much
about him today; he has paid
his price and we don't even
bother to laugh anymore.

Mango Seedling

LINE 14: *the widow of infinite faith* refers to the story of the widow of Sarephath in the First Book of Kings, chapter 17.

LINE 18: *Old Tortoise's miraculous feast:* Once upon a time Tortoise went to work for an old woman, and at the end of his labors she set before him a bowl containing a lone cocoyam sitting on a mound of cooked green leaves. Naturally, Tortoise protested vehemently and refused to touch such a meager meal. In the end, however, he was persuaded, still protesting, to give it a try. Then he discovered to his amazement (and nearly his undoing) that another cocoyam always appeared in the bowl as soon as he ate the previous one.

LINE 24: *the primordial quarrel of Earth and Sky:* This was a dispute over who was sovereign. It led finally to Sky's withholding of rain for seven whole years, until the ground became hard as iron and the dead could not be buried. Only then did Earth sue for peace, sending high-flying Vulture as emissary.

Christmas in Biafra (1969)

LINE 30: *new aluminum coins:* A completely unsuccessful effort was made in Biafra to peg galloping prices by introducing new coins of a lower denomination than the paper money that had come in earlier. But it was too late. The market, having already settled for the five-shilling currency note as its smallest medium of exchange, paid no heed to the new coins.

An "If" of History

LINE 5: A Japanese general named Tomayuki Yamashita was hanged by the Americans at the end of the Second World War for war crimes committed by troops under his nominal command in the Philippines.

Remembrance Day

The Igbo people around my hometown, Ogidi, had an annual observance called Ọsọ Nwanadi. On the night preceding it, all able-bodied men in the village took flight and went into hiding in neighboring villages in order to escape the ire of Nwanadi or dead kindred killed in war.

Although the Igbo people admire courage and valor they do not glamorize death, least of all death in battle. They have no Valhalla concept; the dead hero bears the living a grudge. Life is the "natural" state; death is tolerable only when it leads again to life—to reincarnation. Two sayings of the Igbo will illustrate their attitude toward death:

(a) A person who cries because he is sick, what will they do who are dead?
(b) Before a dead man is reincarnated an emaciated man will recover his flesh.

A Wake for Okigbo

This poem is an elaboration of a traditional Igbo dirge.

In some parts of Igbo land the death of a young person was first publicized by members of his or her age grade chanting through the village in a make-believe search for their missing comrade, who they insisted was only playing hide-and-seek with them.

The refrain of their chant, *nzomalizo*, is made up of *zo*, which means *hide*, and *mali*, which is a playful sound. The repeat of *zo* and the linking *mali* complete the effect of *hiding in play*. *Ugboko* is the personification of the tropical forest, while *Iyi* personifies the stream. *Ogbonuke* is the embodiment of ill will and catastrophe.

Love Song (for Anna)

LINE 8: Leaves of cocoyam come in handy for wrapping small and delicate things. For instance, before storage, kola nuts are wrapped in cocoyam leaves to preserve them from desiccation. However, cocoyam leaves are not for rough handling as Vulture learned to his cost when he received from the hands of an appeased Sky a bundle of rain wrapped in them to take home to drought-stricken Earth.

Beware, Soul Brother

LINE 10: *abia* drums beaten at the funeral of an Igbo titled man. The dance itself is also called *abia* and is danced by the dead man's peers while he lies in state and finally by two men bearing his coffin before it is taken for burial; so he goes to his ancestors by a final *rite de passage* in solemn paces of dance.

Misunderstanding

The Igbo people have a firm belief in the duality of things. Nothing is by itself, nothing is absolute. "I am the way, the Truth, and the Life" would be meaningless in Igbo theology. They say that a man may be right by Udo and yet be killed by Ogwugwu; in other words, he may worship one god to perfection and yet fall foul of another.

Igbo proverbs bring out this duality of existence very well. Take any proverb that puts forward a point of view or a "truth" and you can always find another that contradicts it or at least puts a limitation on the absoluteness of its validity.

Lazarus

LINE 12: *Ogbaku:* Many years ago a strange and terrible thing happened in the small village of Ogbaku. A lawyer driving on the highway that passes by that village ran over a man. The villagers, thinking the man had been killed, set upon the lawyer and clubbed him to death. Then to their horror, their man began to stir. So, the story went, they set upon him too and finished him off, saying, "You can't come back having made us do that."

Those Gods Are Children

The attitude of Igbo people to their gods is sometimes ambivalent. This arises from a worldview that sees the land of the spirits as a territorial extension of the human domain. Each sphere has its functions as well as its privileges in relation to the other. Thus a man is not entirely without authority in dealing with the spirit world nor entirely at its mercy. The deified spirits of his ancestors look after his welfare; in return he regularly offers them sustenance in the form of sacrifice. In such a reciprocal relationship one is encouraged (within reason) to try to get the better of the bargain.

Lament of the Sacred Python

LINE 10: *acknowledged my face in broken dirges:* One of the songs that
accompany the dead to the burial place at nightfall has these
lines:

> Look a python! Look a python!
> Python lies across the way!

LINE 24: *creation's day of gifts:* We all choose our gifts, our character,
our fate from the Creator just before we make our journey into
the world. The sacred python did not choose (like some other
snakes) the terror of the fang and venom, and yet it received a
presence more overpowering than theirs.

Their Idiot Song

The Christian claim of victory over death, is to the unconverted vil-
lager, one of the really puzzling things about the faith. Are these
Christians just naive or plain hypocritical?

He Loves Me; He Loves Me Not

Lines provoked by the news that a street in the Nigerian city of Port
Harcourt had been named after Britain's prime minister Harold Wilson.

Dereliction

This poem is in three short movements. The first is the inquirer
(onye ajuju); the second, the mediating diviner (dibia), who frames the
inquiry in general terms; and the third is the Oracle.

We Laughed at Him

LINE 36: *wild avenging demons:* This refers to the story of Tortoise and
the miraculous food drum offered him in spirit land in com-
pensation for his palm nut that one of the spirit children has
eaten. After long use (and misuse) the drum ceases to produce
any more feasts when it is beaten. Whereupon Tortoise bla-
tantly contrives a reenactment of his first visit to spirit land.
But this time the spirits (fully aware, no doubt, of his greed)
take him to a long row of hanging drums and allow him to
pick one for himself. As you would expect, he picks the largest
and lumbers away under its great weight. Home at last, he
makes elaborate arrangements for a feast and then beats the
drum. No food comes; instead demons armed with long whips
emerge and belabor him to their satisfaction.

The element of choice is a recurrent theme in Igbo folklore,
especially in man's dealings with the spirit world. We are not
forced; we make a free choice.